WHEN WORLDS COLLIDE

WHEN WORLDS COLLIDE

WHERE IS GOD?

R. C. SPROUL

::: CROSSWAY

WHEATON, ILLINOIS

When Worlds Collide: Where Is God?

Copyright © 2002 by R. C. Sproul

Published by Crossway
    1300 Crescent Street
    Wheaton, Illinois 60187

Cover design: Kyle Shuflin, www.kyleshuflin.us

Cover photo: Corbis Images

First printing 2002

Reprinted with new cover 2011

Printed in the United States of America

Trade Paperback ISBN: 978-1-4335-2753-1

Scripture references are from the *New King James Version.* Copyright © 1982, Thomas Nelson, Inc. Used by permission.

Library of Congress Cataloging-in-Publication Data
Sproul, R. C. (Robert Charles), 1939–
 When worlds collide : where is God? / R. C. Sproul.
  p. cm.
 Includes index.
 ISBN 1-58134-442-2 (alk. paper)
 1. Providence and government of God. 2. September 11 Terrorist
Attacks, 2001. I. Title.
BT96.3 .S67   2002
231'.5—dc21   2002009545

Crossway is a publishing ministry of Good News Publishers.

V P 20 19 18 17 16 15 14 13 12 11
15 14 13 12 11 10 9 8 7 6 5 4 3 2 1

CONTENTS

1

A War of Ideas

As I am writing, the United States of America is at war. It is possible that by the time you read this book the war will be over. I certainly hope that will be the case, but we have been told by our president that we should anticipate a long and protracted effort, as we are engaged in an unusual kind of warfare. We've been told that the United States is not involved in a conventional war against a particular nation or against a particular ethnic group or against a particular religion. Rather this has been defined as a war on terrorism. It is a war where the enemy is elusive. He appears and disappears as a phantom. There are no phalanxes of soldiers, no fleets of ships, no organized squadrons of bombers or fighter planes. Our own planes are hijacked and used as weapons against us.

The targets are not necessarily military bases. The World Trade Center towers were quite different from our naval base at Pearl Harbor. Civilians, not soldiers, were hit in New York. That's the method of terrorism. It is coldly calculated to achieve its objective of terror. It is shrewdly designed to provoke fear and paralysis. It intends to cripple a nation.

The terrorist wants us to think there is a bomb on every plane, anthrax in every letter, a sniper in every tree. He wants us to believe that no one is safe, that there is no refuge from his violence.

Terrorism is a war of the mind, designed to get to the nerves and the will. It is a different kind of war with a different kind of conquest in view.

Even "traditional" warfare evokes terror in the human heart, as we all know. I was a young boy during World War II. My father was overseas, fighting in North Africa. We lived in a suburban community far removed from the battlefields of Europe, Africa, and the Pacific. Still, our house was furnished with black shades to cover the windows during the blackouts that were a routine part of our lives. When the air-raid whistle blew, it signaled time to extinguish lights and pull down the black shades. The idea was to conceal land targets in the event of an enemy bombing raid. The air-raid warden would walk down our street to make sure that no lights were visible and that the civilian population was complying with air-raid instructions.

We lived a short distance from what was then the main commercial airport serving Pittsburgh. The glide path for landing planes came right over our house. When the air-raid siren blew, my mother would tuck me into bed and sit with me during the drill. I still remember lying in the dark listening to the sound of airplanes flying overhead. I had no concept of the difference between practice and reality. The experience was one of ice-cold terror as I waited for the bombs to explode on our house. For children in England and other places in the world, the air raids were real. I can hardly imagine the terror they experienced.

To terrorize people is to paralyze them. It is to cripple their economy, rob them of the joy of travel, and keep them ever frightened from performing the simple acts of normal daily life such as shopping, riding a bus, or eating in a restaurant. Even churches are no longer places of "sanctuary," refuges from cold-blooded attacks.

This kind of evil not only allows for war, it demands it. Terrorists must be rooted out of their lairs and made to pay for their inhuman actions. President Bush was right when he insisted that not only the terrorists themselves but also nations that harbor and export terrorism must be brought to account.

THE ROOTS OF WAR

What causes wars such as our present war on terrorism? Historians say World War I was caused by the assassination of an Austrian archduke in the Balkans. World War II, at least the United States' involvement in it, was provoked by an attack on Pearl Harbor. We can go back even earlier in our own history to the artillery attack on Fort Sumter that provoked the conflict we call the Civil War. And before that, the "shot heard 'round the world," fired by a patriot Minuteman in Massachusetts, provoked the American Revolutionary War.

However, the moments of crisis that historians freeze-frame as the events that tip the scales of peace to the side of war cannot in themselves explain the outbreak of war. Rather they were the points of eruption for the sudden release of pent-up hostility, the boiling point of waters already heated and churned. To understand the deeper causes of these epoch-making conflicts, one must search more deeply, probing beyond the superficial veneer of physical points of collision. We must penetrate to the mind to get to the root cause of wars. There we look for ideas in conflict—for the crashing together of conflicting philosophies.

Many wars have been fought because people differed radically on what form of government they should have, how that government should be structured, or how it should function. Political ideology has produced innumerable physical conflicts. There have been other occasions where war has been provoked by economic considerations—how commercial activity is to be handled—or how religious expressions are to be maintained or in some cases suppressed.

In the twentieth century, more than two billion people were enslaved inside what Winston Churchill described as the "Iron Curtain." Millions perished in wars and political purges that sought either to advance or to retard the spread of communism. The hammer and the sickle became symbols for a movement of world domination. But this movement did not begin in Russia or in China. Its architect was neither Joseph Stalin nor Mao Tse-tung. The communist dream began in London. It began in the British Museum, where a young German student forged the ideas that were later to bear his name. Marx's ideas were hostile to the ideas of capitalism. The two ideologies were bound to collide, and when and where they did, cultures were torn asunder and structures of society were thrown into upheaval.

DO WE ALL BELIEVE THE SAME THING?

When we talk about the conflict of ideas, we are describing a collision between worldviews. The term *worldview* defines how people understand their position, their significance, and their place on this planet. There are three main ingredients that make up one's worldview. These include 1) our understanding of God, 2) our understanding of mankind, and 3) our understanding of the world. These ideas incorporate within them an understanding of the relationship between God and man, between man and this world, and between this world and God. These are the crucial facets of our self-understanding as human beings.

Since the September 11 attacks on the United States, there has been much public discussion about the role of God in our lives, and we have seen an unprecedented response of the American people in prayer and public worship. Suddenly, the God who had been exiled from the public square, who had been banished to the other side of the wall that separates church and state, was called upon to get back into the game. It became fashionable for the nation to stage religious rallies featuring film stars, politicians, and clerics. Televised worship services called upon the nation to put aside theological differences and come together in a show of religious unity. Ecumenism got a shot in the arm as cooperation went beyond interdenominational Christian worship to worship among people of entirely different religions. The upside of renewed religious zeal was matched with the downside of syncretism.

Religious syncretism involves the mixing or blending together of elements from different religions in an attempt to achieve unity. It is seen, for example, in the marriage of Roman Catholicism and voodooism in Haiti, and of New Age ways of thinking with Christianity in America. It was the plague of Old Testament Israel that reached its nadir during the reign of Ahab, when his consort Jezebel imported priests of Baal and constructed temples for them in the heart of Israel.

America is the perfect place for religious syncretism to flourish. Here it is axiomatic that the many should become one. Indeed our very currency proclaims it—*E Pluribus Unum*. America is the "melting pot" of people not only of different national and ethnic backgrounds but also of different religious backgrounds.

American syncretism is often presumed when we take a short step or make a facile inference from our constitution's first amendment, which guarantees the free exercise of religion. This freedom is granted not only to Christians and Jews but to people of any religious persuasion. We take pride in the freedom of religion in our country. We have enshrined the principle that all religions have equal protection under the law. The civil law of the United States of America grants religious freedom to Buddhists, Hindus, Muslims, Jews, Christians, Protestants, Catholics, and many other religions as well. In the wake of that guarantee of religious freedom has come the idea, deeply rooted in American culture, that because all religions are equal in terms of their protection under the law, therefore all religions are equally valid.

This inference is, of course, gratuitous. The constitution does not and cannot demonstrate the equal truth or validity of all religions. In guaranteeing equal freedom of religious expression as a legal right, the constitution guarantees the right of the individual to be committed to a false religion. But this right, granted by the state, is not granted by God. Our civil "rights" do not always match up with our divine obligations. The very first commandment of the Decalogue, in sharp contrast to the first amendment of the U.S. constitution, requires *exclusive* worship of Yahweh as the only true God. In His presence and under His rule, other religions are considered idolatry and are exposed to His wrath.

We have seen several community worship services that have featured representatives from Catholicism, Protestantism, Islam, Judaism, and other religions. The news commentators tell us repeatedly how wonderful it is that people from these different religious groups come together to pray for God's mercy on our nation. "After all," they say, "we all believe in the same God." People think that, though we are praying and carrying out our religious activities in slightly different forms, and though we come from different traditions, at the bottom we all believe the same thing and are praying to the same God.

But even a cursory glance at the content of world religions reveals that there are radical differences among the various religions.

A recent television talk show featured a discussion between a Protestant Christian and a Jewish rabbi. In that discussion, the moderator was saying that their two views were basically the same. I couldn't help but think how strange this was. It certainly keeps peace and preserves American unity, but is there no difference between an affirmation of Jesus of Nazareth as the long-awaited Messiah of Israel, and the *denial* of that premise? Is it possible that Jesus could be at the same time the true Messiah and Redeemer of His people and *not* the Messiah but a false teacher? Those positions cannot possibly both be true. Nor can they be reconciled with each other. The only way we can say that Judaism and Christianity at root are the same is if we completely ignore the central position of Jesus to the Christian faith. The first affirmation of Christianity is the affirmation that Jesus is the Christ, which is the Greek word for Messiah. That is a distinction that distinguishes two great religions, and it is a huge difference.

DO WE ALL WORSHIP THE SAME GOD?

What about the idea that we all believe in the same God? If we study the Christian concept of God and put it next to the Buddhist concept of God, we will see a radical difference in the theology. If we place the Christian concept of God next to the teachings of the Koran, we will see that the Father of the Lord Jesus Christ has very little in common with the Islamic concept of Allah.

But don't Judaism and Christianity both come from the Bible? Certainly, then, they must worship the same God? No, they do not.

This was the dispute Jesus had with the Jewish authorities of His own day:

Therefore the Jews sought all the more to kill Him, because He not only broke the Sabbath, but also said that God was His Father, making Himself equal with God. Then Jesus answered and said to them, "Most assuredly, I say to you, the Son can do nothing of Himself, but what He sees the Father do; for whatever He does, the Son also does in like manner. For the Father loves the Son, and shows Him all things that

He Himself does; and He will show Him greater works than these, that you may marvel. For as the Father raises the dead and gives life to them, even so the Son gives life to whom He will. For the Father judges no one, but has committed all judgment to the Son, that all should honor the Son just as they honor the Father. He who does not honor the Son does not honor the Father who sent Him" (John 5:18-23).

The heart of the Christian worldview is a concept essential to Christianity, the idea that God is triune. If there is anything that classical Judaism categorically rejects, it is any idea of trinity. Since this is so manifest, how can a thinking person say that Christians and Jews worship the same God? In fact, our understandings of God are on a collision course. And how we understand God is the most crucial ingredient of how we understand ourselves and how we understand the world. The most significant element to the construction of a worldview is our understanding of the nature of God.

This idea swims against the strong tide of public opinion. What I'm saying here is politically incorrect because American civil religion teaches as its central axiom that all religions are the same and that everyone is worshiping the same God. But Christianity says, "No, we do not worship the same God." Step back for a moment to the pages of the Old Testament. Consider the experience of the people of Israel, who entered into a special covenant relationship with their God, Yahweh, and embraced monotheism. When they interacted with their neighbors, they were constantly involved in the problem of syncretism. They would borrow elements from the pagan religions that surrounded them and try to incorporate them into their worship. In so doing, they were violating the first commandment that God gave to Israel through Moses: "You shall have no other gods before Me" (Exodus 20:3).

Nothing is more "un-American" than to have an exclusive understanding of God. Yet nothing is more fundamental to the biblical concept of monotheism than the exclusivity of the God of heaven and earth. In 1 Kings 18 we read of the prophet Elijah engaging in a contest with the priests of Baal on Mount Carmel. But try to imagine Elijah giving an interview to the media assembled to watch this contest. Imagine him speaking into a microphone, saying, "Well, you know, at the end of the day, I and the prophets of Baal really worship the same God. We believe in the same religion. We just do it differently. Our religious activity is not the same. There are elements in the religion of Baal that are different from the elements of the religion of Israel, but surely the God of Israel doesn't mind. In fact, He's honored when we celebrate our religious unity."

Can you imagine anything more foreign to the teaching of sacred Scripture than that? It has been said by biblical scholars that the greatest weakness that led to the destruction of the Jewish nation in the Old Testament was not a military weakness but a theological weakness. What got the people of Israel in trouble with God over and over again was the blending and mixing of their God-given faith with pagan religion.

If we look at the first chapter of Romans, we see that the primordial sin that defines all subsequent human sin is the human penchant for idolatry, for distorting the concept of God. This act of distortion is not limited to pagan religions. It can creep into the Christian religion as well. When we distort or reject aspects of God's self-revelation, we fall into the sin of idolatry (Romans 1:18-25).

We cannot assume that everyone believes in the same God—because they don't. According to the Scriptures, there are few who have a sound and truly biblical understanding of the character of God. The Christian's question for himself should not be, "Does everyone else in the world follow the true God?" but rather, "Do I? Am I consistent in my thinking and in my living with the God who is?"

How we understand God has a profound impact on how we understand ourselves. Both Christianity and the Old Testament Jewish faith from which it arose assert that we are created in the image of God. If we have an incorrect understanding of the archetype (God), we will misunderstand and distort the type (mankind) that is based on it. If we don't know who God is, how can we know what it means to be in His image? If the copy or the image is called to reflect the original, then how we understand the original will determine how we understand our duty to reflect Him in our lives.

9/11 SHOWS THE REALITY OF EVIL

One of the things that I am grateful for as a consequence of the tragedy that befell the United States on 9/11 is something we began to hear on television. Suddenly it was politically acceptable for the media to speak of real, objective evil. Indeed, when I watched the buildings implode, I knew we had marked a turning point of moral relativism in American history. The events of 9/11 were a mortal blow to relativism, because the response of Americans and the response of people the world over, after looking at this heinous attack on human life, was the very "unrelativistic" declaration that "This is evil."

Recently I saw that same affirmation made by a national news service, where a headline bulletin on the screen proclaimed, "The end of moral relativism." One cannot have such a shocking encounter with pure evil and walk away, saying, "Well, it's a relative thing."

9/11 SHOWS THE VALUE OF HUMAN LIFE

We witnessed on 9/11 the absolute wickedness of an assault on human life. We also saw, with the implosion of those buildings, the practical end of macroevolution as a defining theory for the human species. Who really believes anymore that mankind is merely a grown-up germ? Who believes anymore that we are nothing but cosmic accidents emerging fortuitously from the slime and destined for annihilation? If we truly believe that, when we see pictures of thousands of people destroyed by an act of violence, it should merely make us yawn. The mass destruction of grown-up germs who have no eternal significance is no more important than going into our yard and using a cherry bomb to blow up an anthill.

But every human being in America knows that he or she is not an ant. Every person on this planet knows that he or she is not a germ. We all know that human life is sacred and that human life is meaningful, which it could not be if there were no purpose for human existence, as macro-evolutionists believe.

If God does not exist, there is no purpose to human existence. We would be, as Jean-Paul Sartre said, nothing more than a "useless passion." [1] But if we understand the existence of God and relate our own existence to His existence, we know that every human life is of great value. We know that human life matters. We know that it matters ultimately that human beings were murdered in the World Trade Center and at the Pentagon and on the four planes that went down on that day.

DID 9/11 ALSO SHOW THE PROVIDENCE OF GOD?

A crucial part of one's worldview is the question of how God relates to this planet, that is, how God relates to mankind and to nature. In our age, we have a tendency to view nature as functioning independently from any governance or rule by God. Prior to 9/11, the concept of divine providence had virtually disappeared from our vocabulary. Christianity affirms that in God "we live and move and have our being" (Acts 17:28). This means that nothing can move, nothing can live, nothing can exist apart from the power of God. If we remove that understanding of God from the equation, we see a universe that operates according to its own internal laws. The scientist replaces the priest as the mediator of human existence and of human meaning. In a world like this, chance, not God, rules the affairs of history. When an apple falls to the ground from a tree branch, we explain this action as being the result of the "law" of gravity. Gravity is seen as a force that operates completely by its own power, utterly independent of the power and sovereignty of God. This is a godless view of nature, where nature itself usurps the role of the Creator and Governor of the universe.

It is clear that how we understand God will determine how we understand nature. In biblical times, people understood the difference between God and nature. Israel had no storm god or fertility god or god of war. The storm was not to be worshiped. Nor was the harvest. For Israel there was one God, and He was the God who ruled over the storm and who reigned over the harvest. No water fell apart from Him; no crops grew without His power.

God is also sovereign in the affairs of mankind. And as we shall see in the following chapters, not even an event such as 9/11 can happen apart from His providence.

2

PEACE
AND CALAMITY

THERE IS A WORD with a rich history in the English language that has all but disappeared from our vocabulary. It vanished long ago from the secular mind-set and is now almost completely absent from Christian discussion as well. It is the word *providence*. If we could journey back one or two hundred years and eavesdrop on the American people of those days, we would hear this word sprinkled liberally throughout their conversation. Personal letters from the past that have survived to this day attest to this fact. People used the word *providence* so often that it became not merely a word that described the activity of God but a name for Him as well. When spelled with an initial capital letter, *Providence* clearly referred to God Himself.

DEISM AND THE BANISHMENT OF GOD

The eighteenth century saw the rise of a religious philosophy called deism. This "religion" never really became an organized movement, but its influence persists even today. At the heart of deism was the assumption that the "God-hypothesis" was necessary to explain the origin of the universe. God was posited as the "first cause" of all things, reflecting the ancient view of Aristotle's "unmoved mover." But this God who made all things stepped out of the picture once His work of creation was finished. The deists used the "clock maker" analogy as their favorite metaphor. God was like a cosmic designer who fashioned an intricate clock. The clock was framed with springs and gears. God wound up the clock, started it ticking, and then left it to run down according to its own internal mechanism. He left it to run by its own internal laws, laws that inhere within the system of nature and govern its entire behavior. The universe is a *closed* system, according to the deists, and not even God can intrude or interfere with its operation.

The God of deism was a God who *created* the universe but did not sustain it by His power nor exercise any government over it. He was, as Will Durant once described Aristotle's God, a "do-nothing king," who "reigns, but does not rule."[2]

Deism banished the idea of God's being actively engaged in the universe and in human history. The deists sent Providence into exile. And as we have noted, though deism never really became an organized religion, its central idea has persisted deeply in the American psyche. On the practical level, the view of God held by most Americans today is not the biblical view of God and His providence but is at best a deistic understanding of God. It is a view of a God who is isolated from the daily affairs of this world—a God who has no providence.

In our lifetime we have seen the banishment of God from the public square. He is not to be spoken of in the domain of public education. We have chosen what we call a religiously "neutral" education, a notion that is manifestly impossible. Every educational curriculum has a philosophical framework. A program of education is conducted either within the framework of theism or against the framework of theism. There is no neutral ground. The current situation in America is that God is not permitted in the educational arena or in the arena of government. Religion is still protected by our first amendment, of course. But in reality what gets protected today is *personal* religion, as long as it is contained on a cultural reservation, outside the sphere of everyday life. Religion is viewed as something for the edification of the soul, for personal strength, but with no bearing on things like economics or government or education. That is deism with a vengeance. God's relevance is restricted to the private and personal sphere. He has no place in the public square.

BRINGING GOD BACK, TO BLESS AMERICA

But the calamity that struck our nation on September 11, 2001, has recalled God from the reservation. Instantly we saw all spheres of American culture rushing to call upon God. The group that was most silent in the initial days and weeks following the disaster was the American Civil Liberties Union. They had long been busy with their court cases in the schools, government, and public square, when suddenly the nation said no to deism and cried out once more for the reaffirmation of divine providence.

With this national change of heart came a three-word slogan that was broadcast everywhere. It appeared in signs, on bumper stickers, on windows, and was quoted by millions as our national plea: "God bless America."

"God bless America" has become a societal mantra. It is the prayer cried out by people gripped in the vise of terrorism. Let us consider for a moment the assumptions contained in this three-word prayer.

"God bless America" assumes that there is such a place as "America." There is no dispute about that. It also assumes that there is such a being as God. These two points are obvious. But the critical word in this three-word phrase is the word *bless*. A deist has no room for a God who has either the capacity or the desire to bless a nation. For God to bless a nation, He has to be involved in its affairs. For God to bless America, He has to exercise His sovereign power over what is going on in the world. What are we asking for when we get on our knees and say, "Please, God, bless America"? We are asking God to intervene. We're asking God to intrude for our nation's well-being. We're asking God to step into this calamity and bring redemption out of it.

DOES GOD ONLY BLESS?

As a Christian and a theologian, I am delighted that the nation is calling upon God for His blessing. But there is much confusion about this. While it is now politically correct to ask God to bless America, we reject the idea that God could have been involved in any way in the tragedy itself. We allow for God's providence as long as it is a blessing, but we have no room for God's providence if that providence represents some kind of judgment. If we look carefully at the biblical understanding of God and construct our worldview on this basis, we see that God in His providence is a sovereign God, who not only governs nature and the laws of nature but who raises nations up and brings nations low. Within His providence come both blessing and calamity.

Let us examine a famous text that deals with this matter. In chapter 45 of Isaiah we read:

> And Israel My elect,
> I have even called you by your name;
> I have named you, though you have not known Me.
> I am the LORD, and there is no other;
> There is no God besides Me.
>
> (vv. 4-5)

> I am the LORD, and there is no other;
> I form the light and create darkness,
> I make peace and create calamity;
> I, the LORD, do all these things.
>
> (vv. 6-7)

Contrary to what this passage teaches, we in America in 2002 have allowed God to come only halfway off the reservation. We have said, "Yes, there is a place for God in nature. There is a place for God in history. There is a place for God among the affairs of human beings." But that place is restricted to blessing. We have no room in our thinking for God's involvement in calamity. But we cannot have it both ways. Deism falls off one side of the horse by saying that God is not responsible for blessing. American humanism falls off the other side of the horse when it says that God may be involved in blessing but could never be involved in calamity.

THE SOVEREIGN GOD OF PEACE AND WAR

But if God is God, then He is sovereign over all things. I have frequently taught a seminary course on the theology of the Westminster Confession of Faith. The third chapter of the Confession always provokes a strong response from students. It begins with these words:

> . . . from all eternity, God doth freely and immutably, according to His own wise counsel, ordain whatsoever comes to pass;

People are often aghast when they see or hear these words. They often dismiss them as merely the harsh teachings of Calvinism or Reformed theology. But there is nothing in the statement unique to Calvinism. Indeed the affirmation is not even unique to Christianity. It is an affirmation found in the tenets of Judaism and also in Islam. All three of these world religions would affirm that (at least in some sense) God ordains whatever comes to pass.

If God did not ordain all things, He would not be sovereign over all things. And if He is not sovereign over all things, then He is not God at all. Theologians argue endlessly over *how* God ordains all things. But even if this ordination is by mere "permission," for God to let things happen that do happen He must *choose* to allow them to take place. Insofar that He lets things happen that He has the power and authority to prevent from happening, He is "ordaining" them.

DIVINE SOVEREIGNTY, HUMAN AGENCY

After the semicolon in the above quote from the Westminster Confession we read, "but not in such a way as to do violence to the will of the creature or to eliminate secondary causes." God's ordination of all things does not annihilate human decisions or the forces of nature. Yet at the same time the sovereignty of God stands over every human event. If I am asked, "Did God ordain the calamity in New York City?" I say, "Yes, He did." Now, if I am asked *why* He ordained it, I cannot be glib in my reply. I could leap to the conclusion that He ordained it to punish America. But as possible as that may be, I cannot rush to such a judgment. In reality, I do not know why God ordained 9/11, but I know that He did ordain it because if He did not ordain it, it would not have happened. Since it happened, I know for certain that God ordained it in some sense. That is one of the most difficult concepts even for devout Christians to deal with. Yet the concept is found on almost every page of sacred Scripture. It is at the very heart of the Christian faith.

Let us examine a passage from the second chapter of the book of Acts, where we have a record of Peter's sermon on the day of Pentecost. In verse 22 we read:

> "Men of Israel, hear these words: Jesus of Nazareth, a Man attested by God to you by miracles, wonders, and signs which God did through Him in your midst, as you yourselves also know—Him, being delivered by the determined purpose and foreknowledge of God, you have taken by lawless hands, have crucified, and put to death; whom God raised up, having loosed the pains of death, because it was not possible that He should be held by it" (Acts 2:22-24).

Peter is giving a severe rebuke to his contemporaries for doing what? For executing Jesus. Even though God had confirmed Christ's identity as the Messiah through His miracles, the people put Him to death. Peter by no means absolves these people of their responsibility for the death of Christ. It was by human hands that Jesus was delivered to Pilate, it was by human hands that He was sentenced to death, and it was by human hands that He was crucified. Yet all of these things, Peter said, did not take place through accidents of human history; rather they took place according to the "determined purpose and foreknowledge" of Almighty God. Before anyone raised a finger against Jesus, when He went to the Garden of Gethsemane, He was completely aware of what was going to happen. He knew it was God's will, not the mere will of mortals, that He must carry out.

Jesus had told His disciples only a few days earlier that He was going to go to Jerusalem to be delivered into the hands of wicked men, and that He was going to be beaten and killed (Matthew 16:21; Luke 24:7). When Jesus went to the Garden of Gethsemane and sweat drops of blood in prayer, He begged God to change that plan (Luke 22:41-44), because Jesus knew that these things had been appointed by His Father. From the time of His birth, Jesus' destiny was set out. When Jesus was brought to the temple for dedication, the prophecy was announced that this One would be a sign for the rise and fall of many, and that a sword was going to pierce the soul of Mary (Luke 2:34-35).

Years before Jesus was put to death, the Word of God revealed that it was God's plan that Jesus should die, and that this would happen through the actions of wicked men. Here is God directing His counsel, bringing His will to pass through a divine providence that works through human agency in such a way as not to cancel out the will or the responsibility of the participants.

The clearest example of this combination of divine providence and human agency is in the story of Joseph in the Old Testament. Because of his brothers' jealousy and envy toward him, Joseph was sold into slavery. On the slave block, Joseph was purchased by Potiphar, whose wife then falsely accused him of abuse, for which Joseph was thrown into prison, where he languished for many years. Eventually, God brought a famine to the land, and because the people were starving, Jacob sent his sons down to Egypt to seek relief from the Egyptian storehouses, which ironically had been prepared through the supervision of Joseph, who had been freed from prison and elevated to the office of prime minister of Egypt.

In that poignant moment of the encounter between Joseph and his brothers, when suddenly the brothers recognized Joseph, they were terrified. They feared his vengeance upon them. Joseph, however, shocked them with his mercy. He understood that their intent had been evil. They had had a purpose in mind when they acted. They sinfully chose to deliver Joseph into the hands of those

Midianite traders, and they were responsible for that. But beyond their decision, beyond their choice stood the sovereignty of God and His providence. As Joseph explained to them, "You meant it for evil, but God meant it for good" (Genesis 50:20). Even in the wicked choices of Joseph's brothers, God was at work to bring His perfect counsel to pass in human history.

That is what we believe if we are Christians. Our worldview affirms a divine Providence who governs human history. He doesn't just govern the orbits of the planets. He is sovereign over everything. That's the idea that defines our whole understanding of human life, our whole understanding of economics, our whole understanding of government, our whole understanding of education. It is that concept that is on a collision course with every philosophy in human history that would deny the sovereignty of God over human life. Does that mean that God is sovereign over tragedy? Yes. Does that mean God was sovereign over the events of 9/11? Yes. And the whole question of tragedy, which seems to be a blemish on the record of God's perfect providence, is the question that we will take up in the next chapter.

3

PURPOSE
IN SUFFERING

WE SAW IN CHAPTER 1 that wars—such as America's war on terrorism—are provoked in the final analysis by the conflict of ideas, that war begins in the mind, and hostilities break out when people come to different conclusions on how to live and how to function. We have also seen the erosion of the importance of the concept of divine providence to even the Christian church in our day. Few Christians today understand the historic doctrine of divine providence, and fewer still understand that God is sovereign over evil as well as good.

WAS 9/11 A "SENSELESS TRAGEDY"?

I have noticed, as the media describe the events of September
11, 2001, that they use words such as "catastrophe" or
"calamity" to describe that day. One word I hear perhaps
more often than any other is "tragedy." I am especially con-
cerned when the events of that dark day are described as
a "senseless" tragedy. If we look closely at the phrase, it
becomes obvious that "senseless tragedy" is an oxymoron.
It is a self-contradictory statement, a phrase that makes no
sense. For something to be defined as "tragic" there first
must be some standard of good for it to be deemed tragic
over against. But if things happen in a way that is "senseless," there cannot be anything that is either a tragedy or a
blessing. Each event would simply be meaningless.

The word "tragedy" presupposes some kind of order or
purpose in the world. If the world has purpose and order,
then all that occurs in it is meaningful in some respect.
The idea of a "senseless tragedy" represents a worldview
that is completely incompatible with Christian thought. It
assumes that something happens without purpose or without meaning. If God is God and if He is a God of providence, if He is truly sovereign, then nothing ever happens
that is ultimately senseless. Things may appear to be without purpose or meaning. Their ultimate purpose might
elude us for the present. Yet if we fail to see purpose in

what happens, we must remember that our view of things is limited by our earthly perspective.

An important slogan in theology is *finitum non capax infiniti*. This means that "the finite cannot grasp the infinite." The limit of our comprehension is the earthly perspective. We do not have the ability to see things *sub specie aeternitatis*—"from the eternal perspective."

The eternal perspective belongs to God. He is the infinite One, whose understanding is likewise infinite. If God is truly sovereign—if He rules over all things—then nothing that ever happens is senseless. Events can be senseless only if: 1) God is not sovereign over them; or 2) He Himself is senseless. What would be *truly* senseless is a view of God that regards Him either as not sovereign or as senseless.

SHORT-TERM AND LONG-TERM CONSEQUENCES OF TRAGEDY

But what about the reality of tragedy? Even if tragedies are not senseless, are they not still tragic? We must look at this from two vantage points, but first we must define the term "tragedy." Apart from its reference to a particular form of drama, the term, according to the dictionary, refers to that which may be called "a disastrous event," a "calamity," or a "severe misfortune."

This language could rightly be used to describe the terrorist attacks of 9/11. But we must distinguish between the short-term consequences of the event and the long-term consequences. We must also distinguish between the various persons who are the so-called victims of the event. Could events such as 9/11 be a tragedy for some but a blessing for others?

In our look at the crucifixion of Christ and the disasters that befell Joseph in the Old Testament, we have seen that what seemed tragic in the short term was actually a blessing in the long term. We remember Joseph's words to his brothers:

> "Do not be afraid, for am I in the place of God? But as for you, you meant evil against me; but God meant it for good, in order to bring it about as it is this day, to save many people alive" (Genesis 50:19-20).

Joseph's "tragedy" was ordained of God for a redemptive purpose. It appeared as a senseless tragedy while in actuality it was a divinely appointed event with a redemptive purpose.

That is seen nowhere more clearly than in the cross. Luke records an event that took place after Jesus' crucifixion:

> Now behold, two of them were traveling that same day to a village called Emmaus, which was seven miles from Jerusalem. And they talked together of all these

things which had happened. So it was, while they conversed and reasoned, that Jesus Himself drew near and went with them. But their eyes were restrained, so that they did not know Him. And He said to them, "What kind of conversation is this that you have with one another as you walk and are sad?" Then the one whose name was Cleopas answered and said to Him, "Are You the only stranger in Jerusalem, and have You not known the things which happened there in these days?" And He said to them, "What things?" So they said to Him, "The things concerning Jesus of Nazareth, who was a Prophet mighty in deed and word before God and all the people, and how the chief priests and our rulers delivered Him to be condemned to death, and crucified Him. But we were hoping that it was He who was going to redeem Israel. Indeed, besides all this, today is the third day since these things happened. Yes, and certain women of our company, who arrived at the tomb early, astonished us. When they did not find His body, they came saying that they had also seen a vision of angels who said He was alive. And certain of those who were with us went to the tomb and found it just as the women had said; but Him they did not see." Then He said to them, "O foolish ones, and slow of heart to believe in all that the prophets have spoken! Ought not the Christ to have suffered these things and to enter into His glory?" And beginning at Moses and all the Prophets, He expounded to them in all the Scriptures the things concerning Himself (Luke 24:13-27).

We notice in this conversation that the two men walking with Jesus were described as being sad. When Jesus asked them why they were sad, they recounted to Him the events of the crucifixion. They expressed the poignant feeling, "But we were hoping that it was He who was going to redeem Israel" (Luke 24:21). At the death of Jesus, these men had experienced the utter destruction of their hope. The hope they had placed in Jesus was crushed. The cross had shattered it. To them, at this time, the cross represented the supreme tragedy. It made their previous devotion to Jesus appear to be "senseless."

The hope they expressed was for redemption. They trusted that Jesus was the One who was going to redeem Israel. At first glance, nothing seemed to be further from a redemptive act than Jesus' death on the cross. Pilate certainly did not intend the cross as an act of redemption. The crowds who clamored for Christ's blood did not view the cross as redemptive. And it is obvious that these disciples, looking back on that terrible event, didn't view it that way either.

Jesus went to the Scriptures to show these men, whom He described as "foolish" and "slow of heart to believe," that the Bible made it clear that the cross was not a senseless tragedy but the most important redemptive act in human history. The cross was the point of collision—the intersection where Christian and pagan worldviews hit head-on.

FOR THE CHRISTIAN, THERE IS
NO SENSELESS TRAGEDY

The distinction between short-term and long-term evaluation of events also demands a differentiation between participants. For Judas, the cross was not the financial boon he had expected. For him it was a genuine tragedy. In all probability it was tragic in the final analysis for people like Pontius Pilate and Caiaphas. Yet for all down through the ages who have put their trust in Jesus, the cross is their highest blessing as it turns Black Friday into Good Friday.

Romans 8:28 summarizes it beautifully:

> And we know that all things work together for good to those who love God, to those who are the called according to His purpose.

This verse is not merely a biblical expression of comfort for those who suffer affliction. It is far more than that. It is a radical *credo* for the Christian worldview. It represents the absolute triumph of divine purpose over all alleged acts of chaos. It erases "misfortune" from the vocabulary of the Christian.

God, in His providence, has the power and the will to work *all things* together for good for His people. This does not mean that everything that happens to us is, in itself, good. Really bad things do happen to us. But they are only proximately bad; they are never ultimately bad. That is, they are bad only in the short (proximate) term, never in the long term. Because of the triumph of God's goodness in all things, He is able to bring good for us out of the bad. He turns our tragedies into supreme blessings.

Because of this truth, we are confident that in the ultimate sense there are no senseless tragedies for the believer. However, the other side of the coin is indeed grim. Just as there are no ultimate tragedies for the believer, so for the impenitent unbeliever there are no ultimate blessings. Every good gift God bestows upon the wicked, for which the wicked do not glorify God or acknowledge His goodness with gratitude and worship, becomes a tragedy. The more gifts God gives that are despised by the recipient, the more guilt is incurred, so that, to the wicked, on Judgment Day the gifts of God's kindness become tragedies.

On 9/11, Christians perished. On 9/11, impenitent unbelievers perished. The former were ushered into the presence of Christ. The latter were sent into outer darkness.

One of the pilots whose plane was flown by the terrorists into the World Trade Center was a Christian. I don't know about the other crew members. I know about this pilot because he was a student of mine at Ligonier Ministries. He is mourned by his family and friends. I grieve over his death. But as we weep at our loss, we know that for him it was gain.

SO, WHY DID 9/11 HAPPEN?

When I was in college, I took an introductory course in lab biology. In fact it was called "bonehead biology" because it was the biology course for non-science majors. Probably the only thing I remember from that class was the first lecture. Keep in mind that, in bonehead biology, 99 percent of the students were freshmen. I happened to be a senior. I also happened to be a philosophy major. I had had to defer taking this course because of scheduling conflicts in my freshman year. What stirred my interest in that opening lecture was that the professor said, "Now, as scientists exploring the realm of biology, the one thing we are not interested in is *teleology.*" The word "teleology" comes from the Greek word *telos,* which means "end," "goal," or "purpose." One of the great quests in the history of philosophy is investigation into the meaning and purpose of life. Philosophy seeks the purpose not only of human existence but also of animal existence, of flower existence, of the existence of rocks and everything else. Philosophy is profoundly interested in questions of purpose and meaning. Yet there in this freshmen class on biology, I was told at the outset that questions of teleology were ruled out of bounds. What I heard the professor say was that "what you will learn from now on in the rest of this course will be meaningless"—meaning was not the concern of his class. The professor was really saying that he was going to limit our investigation to questions of *how* and *what* and *where,* but the one question that would be ruled out of bounds was the question *why.*

But when we return to the events of September 11, 2001, this is the question that burns in everyone's mind. *Why* did this happen? Particularly if one is a theist and especially a Christian theist, we are asking the why question. "How could God allow this to happen?" or "Why, God, did this happen?" Christians do not allow for meaningless events to take place, because at the heart of the Christian worldview is the idea that everything in history has a purpose in the mind of Almighty God. God is a purposive God; He is not chaotic. As Albert Einstein once remarked, God does not "play dice" with the universe.[3] For everything there is a purpose—including what we define as tragedies. Knowing this, however, we are still pressed to ask the why question.

WAS IT GOD'S JUDGMENT ON AMERICA?

One of the things that took place in the early days of reflection about the events of September 11 were comments from some well-known preachers. Some of them made the observation that the *why* for this tragedy was that it was God's act of judgment upon America for our immorality. They claimed it was judgment for abortion, the destruction of the human family, and other moral issues of our day. This opinion was met by a firestorm of controversy. There was a negative backlash from the press against these Christian leaders. To suggest that the events of 9/11 could be remotely connected to an act of divine judgment was deemed to be the nadir of political incorrectness.

If someone would say to me, "Why did this happen? What was God's purpose in all of this?" the only honest answer I could give would be, simply, "I don't know." I can't read God's mind. If you were to ask me, "Was God involved?" my answer, of course, would be yes. Because I'm committed to the Christian doctrine of providence, I'm convinced that God was involved in this act, that it was according to God's purpose. But what His specific purpose was in this event, I do not know.

I cannot jump to the conclusion that God's purpose on 9/11 was to send judgment on America, but one of the things that disturbed me was how confident the commentators were that it was *not* an act of judgment. Let me say again, I don't *know* that it was an act of judgment, but I cannot think of anything in the Christian worldview that would rule out the possibility that it was an act of judgment. We understand that God does bring calamities from time to time upon nations as acts of judgment. It is to struggle not only with that particular event but with the tragedies that befall people throughout the ages that the question *why* is raised.

HUMAN TRAGEDIES, DIVINE PURPOSES

Let us turn our attention at least briefly to a discussion Jesus had with His disciples, recorded in the ninth chapter of the Gospel of John. We read these words:

> Now as Jesus passed by, He saw a man who was blind from birth (John 9:1).

Let's stop right there for a moment. Let's say you are a mother. You carry your baby to term. You're excited in anticipation of the birth of this child. But soon after the baby is born, you discover that he is blind. Few people would respond to such an experience with joy or would react to that experience as a visitation of divine blessing. In a word, the parents in their disappointment, in all probability, would see that event, at least for them and for their child, as a personal tragedy. And certainly people would be inclined to ask, "Why, God, did You let this happen?"

The disciples of Jesus met a blind person when he was a grown adult. They knew that he had been born blind, suffering total blindness for many years. If anything seems senseless, it is the experience of a man born blind. So the disciples came to Jesus and asked Him, "Rabbi, who sinned, this man or his parents, that he was born blind?" (v. 2).

Jesus immediately recognized that the question posed to Him committed a logical fallacy, for which we have a technical name. It is the fallacy of the false dilemma, sometimes called the either/or fallacy. The fallacy is committed when a person reduces possibilities or options to two and only two, when in fact there may be more possibilities. There *are* situations when the possibilities can legitimately and rationally be reduced to two. For instance, either there is a God or there is not a God. There's no third alternative. It's one or the other. You are either going to die or you are not going to die. But in this case, the disciples rushed to judgment and reduced the options to two when there was a third option they hadn't considered. So Jesus, when He heard the question stated this way, answered by saying, "Neither."

> Jesus answered, "Neither this man nor his parents sinned, but that the works of God should be revealed in him" (John 9:3).

This man had been born blind so many years before, so that, on this particular day, God's kingdom could be manifested through his healing. God's purpose here was to demonstrate who Jesus was. And to this day, 2,000 years later, that blind man, who presumably is in heaven today and perhaps has been joined by his children and grandchildren, sits with them and talks about how God used his blindness to demonstrate the identity of Christ. He discovered that his tragic condition was by no means senseless. It had a divine purpose that has borne witness to Christ through all history.

SIN AND SUFFERING

We look at the story of the man born blind and see that the disciples made a mistake. They rushed to judgment, assuming that the only possible explanations for the man's lifelong blindness were either the man's sin or his parents' sin. The disciples were wrong. But let's not dismiss them as being stupid. Some people read this text and think, *What's wrong with those disciples that they would think that God would allow a child to be born blind because of the parents' sin, or that the man was stricken with blindness because of some sin that he himself had committed?* Why did these disciples of Jesus, who had been to the finest "theological seminary" in the history of the world, make that assumption?

They had been trained by the Word of God Himself. Why would they assume that there was some kind of relationship between sin and suffering? They assumed this because they knew the truth of God, that the ultimate reason for tragedy, the ultimate reason for suffering in this world, is sin. If you rid the world of sin, you will rid it of suffering. In heaven there is no sin, and in heaven there is no death.

The disciples understood that there is a link in this world between sin and suffering, between evil and tragedy. But they made the mistake of assuming that the cause for this tragedy was a particular sin of a particular person. Had they read carefully the book of Job, they would have known better. Remember the misery of Job? It is presented to us in this exquisitely insightful piece of wisdom literature. The book of Job opens as a drama opens, with a first act and a first scene where Satan comes before God after he had walked to and fro on the earth . . .

> Then the LORD said to Satan, "Have you considered My servant Job, that there is none like him on the earth, a blameless and upright man, one who fears God and shuns evil?" So Satan answered the LORD and said, "Does Job fear God for nothing? Have You not made a hedge around him, around his household, and around all that he has on every side? You have blessed the work of his hands, and his possessions have increased in the land. But now, stretch out Your hand

and touch all that he has, and he will surely curse You to Your face!" And the LORD said to Satan, "Behold, all that he has is in your power; only do not lay a hand on his person." So Satan went out from the presence of the LORD (Job 1:8-12).

When God pointed to Job as a model of obedience, Satan's response was bathed in cynicism. He accused Job of being godly out of impure motives. Satan challenged God to a test to see if Job would renounce his trust in God and curse Him if he were exposed to Satan's attacks. As Job then began to suffer, he didn't know why he was going through misery and relentless pain, but in the agony of his suffering at Satan's hand, he remained faithful, at one point proclaiming of God, "Though He slay me, yet will I trust Him" (Job 13:15).

Job's friends came to this faithful man armed with their beliefs about the relationship between sin and suffering. They suspected that Job was caught up in some secret sin. They drew the inference that since Job was in gross pain he must also be in gross guilt. They thought there must be an equation between his sinfulness and his guilt. The whole book of Job is written to disprove that conclusion and that assumption.

The purpose of Job's suffering had nothing to do with his personal guilt. His friends had made that assumption because they knew that, at times in history, God does visit judgment on people and afflict them with pain and suffering as an execution of justice. David spent seven days on his face, in sackcloth and ashes, praying that God would spare the life of the baby born as a result of his sin with Bathsheba. The prophet Nathan had informed David that God was going to take the life of that child in judgment. Yet David still pleaded with God, for an entire week, to spare the baby. But the Bible tells us that God took the child, as judgment upon David (2 Samuel 12:14-18). Even a cursory reading of the Old Testament Scriptures shows that the God of Israel inflicts judgment on people because of their sin. The error of the disciples and the error of Job's friends was assuming that in *every* situation there is a direct correlation between sin and judgment. This is refuted by Jesus' teaching in John 9 and by the entire book of Job.

What was Paul's sin that caused him to have a "thorn in the flesh" (2 Corinthians 12:7)? That thorn was given to him for his own sanctification, to manifest the goodness of God, so that Paul would rely constantly on divine grace (v. 9). There are many reasons why God visits His people with what we call tragedy without its being a direct judgment on sin, though at times it *is* a judgment.

The message of the encounter between Jesus and His disciples regarding the man born blind is that we should not rush to judgment. The man's blindness was not because he was being judged by God or because his parents were being judged by God. If asked why 9/11 happened, the only honest answer I can give is, "I don't know."

"YET I WILL REJOICE IN THE LORD"

I must, however, add this. Though we dare not rush to assume that 9/11 was God's judgment on us, we must also not assume that it was not. Billy Graham once remarked, "If God does not judge America, He's going to have to apologize to Sodom and Gomorrah."[4] Our nation has much to repent of. There are manifold reasons for God to judge us. The worst rush to judgment we can indulge in is to assume that God is always on our side. God is always on the side of the righteous. Only when our nation is righteous can we assume that God is our ally.

We must heed the message of the prophet Habakkuk, who struggled with God's using evil nations to punish His own people:

> Are You not from everlasting,
> O LORD my God, my Holy One?
> We shall not die.
> O LORD, You have appointed them for judgment;
> O Rock, You have marked them for correction.
> You are of purer eyes than to behold evil,

And cannot look on wickedness.
Why do You look on those who deal treacherously,
And hold Your tongue when the wicked devours
A person more righteous than he?
Why do You make men like fish of the sea,
Like creeping things that have no ruler over them?

(Habakkuk 1:12-14)

God then showed Habakkuk that, though He sometimes used other nations to discipline His sinful people,
those other nations were subject to His discipline as
well (Habakkuk 2:2-20). Habakkuk responded to this
revelation with a renewed appreciation for God's divine
sovereignty:

When I heard, my body trembled;
My lips quivered at the voice;
Rottenness entered my bones;
And I trembled in myself,
That I might rest in the day of trouble.
When he comes up to the people,
He will invade them with his troops.

Though the fig tree may not blossom,
Nor fruit be on the vines;
Though the labor of the olive may fail,
And the fields yield no food;
Though the flock may be cut off from the fold,

And there be no herd in the stalls—
Yet I will rejoice in the LORD,
I will joy in the God of my salvation.

The LORD God is my strength;
He will make my feet like deer's feet,
And He will make me walk on my high hills.

(Habakkuk 3:16-19)

Like Habakkuk, we should take comfort in God's sovereignty over human affairs. And as we shall see in the final chapters of this book, we can find such comfort even when God displays His righteous wrath.

4

THE GRAPES OF WRATH

THE CULTURE AND "RELIGION" OF AMERICA TODAY

The year was 1968. It was a time of cultural revolution in the United States of America. It was the decade that saw the birth of the free speech movement, the free sex movement, and the agitation to sanction abortion on demand, which was to come about a few years later. It was a time of unprecedented protest against the American government with respect to our engagement in Vietnam.

This cultural revolution was far different from the

armed revolution of the eighteenth century in which the United States won its independence from England. The American Revolution was fought, not to overturn the present forms and structures of American life in the colonies, but to preserve it from serious changes being imposed by the British government. The revolution of the 1960s was a different matter. This revolution struck at the core of traditional American life. Social mores, family values, and cherished ethics were critiqued, attacked, rejected, and disposed of. In its wake came a cultural war that continues to this day.

With the rise of the drug culture in the 60s, two popular slogans were repeated as a mantra for the youth: 1) "Do your own thing"; and 2) "Tell it like it is." The first slogan sought to justify things such as free sex, abortion, and the use of addictive drugs. It was a declaration of independence in the realm of personal ethics. The second slogan was directed to the post-thirty-year-old generation (the "establishment"). They were called upon to face the truth about their own allegedly hypocritical behavior.

When we look at the twin slogans, their mutual contradiction is immediately obvious. The first, "Do your own thing," was a call to moral relativity and pure subjectivism at the ethical level. Individual personal preference became the only "norm" for behavior. The real "unalienable right" of the new "constitution" was the right to do whatever you wanted to do. But the youth culture that fed off the charge against the older generation's hypocrisy showed themselves capable of greatly exceeding their elders in the art of hypocrisy. For to insist that other people "tell it like it is" assumes that there is an objective reality that can be expressed by objective truth. And to thus embrace pure subjectivism for oneself while calling others to objectivism is hypocrisy in the extreme.

The new generation sought subjectivism for themselves while demanding objectivity from others. This represents the built-in folly of the "new ethic." It reveals not so much that the subjectivistic ethic of moral relativism is wicked (which indeed it is) but that it is clearly silly. No one really believes that everyone has a right to do their own thing. They can't believe it. When a thief's "thing" is to steal your car, you cry foul because you don't really believe that everyone has a right to do their own thing.

The cultural revolution of the 1960s brought about a transition from Enlightenment modernism, with its appeal to natural law and reason, to what is often called "postmodernism." The twin pillars of postmodernism are relativism and narcissism. Narcissism derives its name from the myth of the Greek youth who fell in love with his own reflection in a pond, which resulted in his being changed into a flower. The spirit of narcissism is "me-ism," wherein my personal desires become the only governing norm for my behavior. My preference, my desire is what counts. No one—not even God—has any right to impose their standards on me.

When abortion on demand is "justified" by an appeal to a woman's "right" over her own body, we wonder where this "right" comes from. If the mother's right annuls the right of the unborn child to live, then society can sanction the murder of the living though yet unborn infant. That such unborn babies are actually "alive" is no longer seriously debated. The medical community routinely refers to the unborn as being alive. Nor can they be considered merely a "part" of the woman's body. Though they are carried within the woman's body, they have their own distinctive and unique DNA "fingerprint," which clearly reveals their individual identity. The basis of the woman's "right" to her own body is found not in natural law nor in biblical law but in moral relativism. The underlying premise is that everyone has a right to do their own thing. The moral justification for abortion comes down to *personal preference*. The woman has the right to abortion because she *prefers* to do that.

Thankfully, this ethical precept has not yet been extended to all forms of human behavior. We still have laws against murder, kidnapping, and the like. But these may be mere relics or vestigial remnants from a previous culture that have not yet yielded to postmodernity. The disintegration of objective morality and law is in a fast-forward mode. There is a general practice of scofflaw at the grass roots of our society. Only yesterday, as I was seated in a restaurant awaiting my meal, I saw a stop sign outside the window. I noticed that people were driving through the stop sign without slowing down, as they had a clear view of traffic patterns ahead of them. Intrigued by this, I began to count. By the time my meal arrived, twenty-three cars had passed the sign and only one had actually stopped. In our culture, stop signs are for other people to get out of my way.

Our postmodern culture has been described as a secular culture, as a neo-pagan culture, and as a neo-barbarian culture. I think the latter description is the most accurate. We tend to think of barbarians as uneducated wild men wearing animal skins, riding horses, and brandishing swords, as they attack pockets of civilized society. They are without courtesy and without conscience. They live by the crude impulses of their basest animalistic appetites. Today our barbarians are different. They are "neo." They have college degrees, wear trendy garments, drive BMWs, and brandish scalpels or gavels rather than swords. But their attacks on civilized society are just as vicious if not more so.

They retain the modicum of objective truth by still insisting that others "tell it like it is." But in terms of personal ethics, "do your own thing" is the rule. It is okay with them that the president of the United States engaged in sexual activity with an intern at the very moment he was on the phone discussing national policy. His personal behavior had no bearing on his function as president. Some were upset when he committed perjury in a court of law— when he failed to "tell it like it is"—but they saw this as a minor offense.

The cultural war with the hosts of postmodernism is real and is almost over. The new culture has clearly won the victory over the old. Postmodernism brings not only a new ethic but a barbarian view of human beings, of nature, and of God. Human beings are viewed as grown-up germs, cosmic accidents whose existence began in primordial soup. They are both soulless and meaningless. When destroyed before birth, they are deemed to be so much domestic garbage. When engaged by the entertainment industry, the media, and now even some churches, humans are often regarded as mindless. They are seen as being moved by impressions, by feelings, and mostly by entertainment. Their sex organs are seen as defining their existence more than are their brains. This barbarian view of humanness believes that people have free will not only in the sense that they are not subject to forces of external coercion but also in the sense that no inherent weakness or evil inclinations influence their decisions. They are free from innate corruption such as that supposed by the Christian doctrine of original sin. Indeed the term "sin" itself is rapidly escaping their vocabulary and is being replaced by phrases such as "making bad choices." Soon, even the descriptive term "bad" for choices will have to give way to a more politically correct term.

The barbarian view of nature believes that all material actions and reactions occur either by sheer chance (a synonym for "nothing") or by built-in independent forces. Nature has no governor above itself. God is denied both as Creator and as Sustainer of His universe. The world lives and moves and has its being in and of itself.

MISSING FROM AMERICAN RELIGION: GOD'S WRATH

Even where God is still acknowledged, He is stripped of His attributes. He is a no-name deity or a multi-named deity who is the same for the Christian, the Jew, the Muslim, and anyone else who wants to be "religious." This God has no resemblance to the God of the Bible. He is a deity without sovereignty, a god without wrath, a judge without judgment, and a force without power.

American civil religion has no place for the reality of God's wrath.

As we saw in chapter 1, the key issues in establishing one's worldview are an understanding of the nature of God and an understanding of the nature of humanity, and of how these two relate. The God of Christianity is a God who is holy. He is a God who is altogether righteous. And He is the God who judges the world. He is a God who reveals His wrath, according to the Scripture, "against all ungodliness and unrighteousness" of mankind (Romans 1:18). The apostle Paul tells us that, as impenitent sinners, we are heaping up wrath, storing it up, treasuring it up against the day of wrath (Romans 2:5). But we don't seem worried about that anymore, because we don't believe in the wrath of God.

With the events following the terrorist attacks on the World Trade Center and the Pentagon, as well as the other events of terrorism that we have known along the way, people rallied behind America, drawing together in a kind of unity, following the slogan, "United we stand." As we observed in chapter 2, the national prayer is now, "God bless America." I've heard many patriotic songs, including "God Bless America." But one particular song that I've heard more often than I've heard it in years is, "The Battle Hymn of the Republic." It was the fight song of the Union army in the Civil War. The song begins with the words, "Mine eyes have seen the glory." The glory of what? "Of the coming of the Lord." Then what follows? "He has trampled out the vintage where the grapes of wrath are stored." The words to "The Battle Hymn of the Republic" are drawn directly from the pages of the New Testament. The words "the grapes of wrath," that also became the title of one of the most well known works of American literature, are drawn from the fourteenth chapter of the book of Revelation.

Let's look at the words John Steinbeck used for his novel *The Grapes of Wrath* and that Julia Ward Howe borrowed for "The Battle Hymn of the Republic":

> Then another angel came out of the temple which is in heaven, he also having a sharp sickle. And another angel came out from the altar, who had power over fire, and he cried with a loud cry to him who had the sharp sickle, saying, "Thrust in your sharp sickle and gather the clusters of the vine of the earth, for her grapes are fully ripe" (Revelation 14:17-18).

As is typical in Revelation, we find here vivid graphic imagery. An angel is seen with a massive sickle, more like a scythe. Another angel tells him to put the sickle into the vine. We see the rows of vines clinging to fences—mature, thick, strong vines filled with plush clusters of grapes. Then the instruction from heaven is to insert the sickle and cut off the very vines that are bearing this luscious fruit. And we read this:

> "Thrust in your sharp sickle and gather the clusters of the vine of the earth, for her grapes are fully ripe." So the angel thrust his sickle into the earth and gathered the vine of the earth, and threw it into the great winepress of the wrath of God (Revelation 14:18b-19).

Are all these vines with their grapes thrown into *a* winepress? No, Scripture doesn't say they are thrown into *a* winepress but into *the great winepress*. That winepress is given further definition and description in the text:

> So the angel thrust his sickle into the earth and gathered the vine of the earth, and threw it into the great winepress of the wrath of God (Revelation 14:19).

The place into which the grapes are thrown is the winepress of divine wrath. Then, the grapes are "trampled outside the city, and blood came out of the winepress, up to the horses' bridles, for one thousand six hundred furlongs" (v. 20). Over this vast distance, blood flows in the streets up to the level of the horses' faces. The grapes represent people who live in constant impenitence and disobedience. God is patient and long-suffering for generation after generation, but He promises that there will be an end to that patience and a time of the visitation of His wrath against human wickedness.

The "grapes of wrath"—we still sing the song, but we don't believe its content.

THE GOD OF WRATH AND MERCY

One of the things that we learn about God in Scripture is that He is the Judge of all of the earth. If a judge eternally tolerates wickedness without exercising judgment, he is not a just judge; he is an unjust judge—he himself is part of the context of evil. God, on the other hand, is not indifferent to the way people commit violence against each other. God is not a passive spectator to all these things. And yet we are tempting Him day and night by our unrestrained wickedness, and He has promised to bring judgment to the world. (As we will see in chapter 5, He also promises a way of escape from that judgment.) We think of September 11, 2001, as the greatest day of calamity in the history of the United States of America, but that day of calamity is not worthy to be compared with the day of calamity that God says will come in the future when the grapes of wrath are thrown into the winepress and are trampled by His judgment.

Notice that the celebration of this event in "The Battle

Hymn of the Republic" is a celebration that is extremely foreign to our cultural way of thinking today. It is a celebration not of the nastiness of God, not of some dark, shadowy, demonic element within God, but rather of His divine glory. "Mine eyes have seen the glory of the coming of the Lord." His coming in judgment is a manifestation of His divine glory, of His divine perfection. We often see the wrath of God as somehow being an impediment to our view of God's character. That's because, in present-day America, our view of God's character is an idol. It is an idol of a God who has been stripped of His true attributes. He's a God who is defined in terms of love and mercy and grace, but we have thrown out any idea of His being just and holy and wrathful. If we are going to be faithful to the biblical understanding of God, we have to understand that He is, among other things, a God of wrath. To be sure, He is also a God of mercy. But the idea of mercy is an empty concept if He has no capacity for wrath.

The only way to understand mercy is against the background of the reality of wrath. When God holds back His wrath, when God circumvents His wrath, then we understand true mercy. If God is incapable of wrath, there can be no mercy because there is nothing from which to be saved.

I recently heard a radio commentator proclaim, "I'm going to say it. In this war against terrorism, God is on our side." He continued, "I know that God is on our side because God is good, and we are good. We are good people."

Rabbi Harold Kushner wrote a best-selling book titled *Why Bad Things Happen to Good People.* The real question is, "Why do good things happen to sinful people such as ourselves?" The Scriptures tell us that there is "none righteous, no, not one" (Romans 3:10). We need to be very careful when we assume that God is on our side, particularly if we make that assumption based on our evaluation of our own goodness. The Scriptures tell us that if the Lord would "mark iniquity," none of us could possibly stand (Psalm 130:3). Salvation is about rescue from the wrath of God, which is a just wrath, a wrath that is deserved.

Let me repeat that at the heart of a Christian worldview stands our understanding of God and our understanding of mankind. If we understand humanity as being essentially, basically, incontrovertibly good, then of course there is no room in our thinking for the wrath of God. For God to be wrathful toward good people would indeed indicate a demonic, dark side to His character. But as we have seen, when the Scriptures speak of God's wrath, it is not a wrath that is revealed against innocence, righteousness, purity, or goodness, but a wrath that is revealed "against all ungodliness and unrighteousness" (Romans 1:18).

If God were to examine my life, He would find enough ungodliness and unrighteousness to be inclined to pick me up, use His sickle to cut me from the earth, and throw me into the winepress of His wrath. That would be completely consistent with His perfection, His holiness, and His glory. But thanks be to God that He has given us a way of salvation by which we can escape His fury. That's what the gospel—and our final chapter—is all about.

5

FINDING PEACE

AT LIGONIER MINISTRIES, our videotape set includes a reproduction of one of the world's most famous statues, Auguste Rodin's *The Thinker.* I have asked our audience, "What is he thinking about?" Some suggest he is thinking about the meaning of life, but according to Rodin, he was trying to capture, in this statue, one deeply involved in the contemplation of hell. Hell is something we are loath to think about. In our previous chapter we considered the reality of the wrath of God, and the ultimate manifestation of that wrath involves the doctrine of hell. The concept of hell has been all but erased from our consciousness. The currently most popular doctrine of salvation is not justification by faith, nor justification by works, but justification by *death*. In this view, all one has to do to be transported into heaven is to die. We have removed from our consciousness any idea that there may be a more grim destination for the human soul than eternal life in heaven.

ANOTHER TIME, ANOTHER TOWER

We have already considered the occasion when the disciples asked Jesus about the tragic experience of the man born blind. In chapter 13 of Luke's Gospel, we see the disciples asking Jesus about another tragedy:

> There were present at that season some who told Him about the Galileans whose blood Pilate had mingled with their sacrifices. And Jesus answered and said to them, "Do you suppose that these Galileans were worse sinners than all other Galileans, because they suffered such things? I tell you, no; . . ." (Luke 13:1-3a).

It is important for us to frame this picture. A tragedy had befallen innocent people. People who were at worship were slaughtered by Pontius Pilate. They were executed in the midst of worship, and their blood was mixed with the sacrifices. Those who heard of this were deeply distressed, and they wanted to know, "How could God allow this to happen?"

Jesus said, "Do you suppose that these Galileans were worse sinners than all other Galileans?" And then He answered His own question: "I tell you, no." We must not draw the inference that the people who were destroyed in this catastrophe were killed because they were guilty and other people were innocent.

I was involved in a train wreck in Alabama in 1993. The train went off a bridge into the water. More people were killed in that train wreck than in all previous Amtrak accidents combined. My wife and I survived, and when we returned to Orlando we were besieged by television reporters and newscasters. They all asked me the same question: "Why do you think God spared you?" My response was that I had no idea, but that I didn't want to make the assumption that I was the "lucky" one. There were Christians who perished in that train wreck, and their next day was spent in far better circumstances than mine. They went immediately to heaven.

That's the kind of question Jesus was asked. Why did the Galilean worshipers die? Jesus' answer is startling:

" . . . unless you repent you will all likewise perish" (Luke 13:3b).

I wonder if Jesus could get away with remarks like that in twenty-first-century America? In the midst of tragedy, instead of bringing comfort and hope, Jesus was saying, "Don't look at those people as being worse than you are, because as long as you maintain a posture of impenitence toward God, you also will perish."

Then Jesus proceeded to the next question:

" . . . Or those eighteen on whom the tower in Siloam fell and killed them, do you think that they were worse sinners than all other men who dwelt in Jerusalem?" (v. 4).

Here was another case of a tower collapsing. In this case it did not kill thousands but only eighteen. Nevertheless, this was tragic enough for people to come to Jesus and question how God could allow this to happen. We might expect Jesus to say something like, "I'm really sorry about that. I know the Bible says that 'He who keeps Israel shall neither slumber nor sleep,' but that's hyperbole. You must understand that God's job of governing and monitoring every molecule in this vast cosmic universe is a taxing job even for deity. Even He has to take a rest from time to time. And on this particular afternoon, while He was catching forty winks, outside of His purview this tower fell on these eighteen people. I'm sorry about that. I'll try to get Him to be more careful in the future."

Or Jesus might have replied, "I told you that there's

not a bird that lands on the earth that God doesn't notice, and that in fact the very hairs of your head are numbered by Him. But on that particular afternoon, He was so busy counting the hairs of a bushy-haired fellow that His attention was diverted from the tower, and it fell." Of course, this is not what Jesus said. He made no attempt to justify God for the presence of tragedy in the world.

OUR INDEBTEDNESS TO GOD

Jesus' worldview was radically different from ours. Jesus had a view of God in which the Father is absolutely perfect in His righteousness and in His justice. He also saw mankind in a radically different way than we do, because Jesus believed that every human being is guilty of sin before God. When someone once addressed Jesus as "Good Teacher," he replied, "Why do you call Me good? No one is good but One, that is, God" (Mark 10:17b, 18). As less than perfectly good people, each of us owes a debt to God that we cannot possibly pay. Jesus gave the same response concerning the collapse of the tower of Siloam as He gave concerning the incident where Pilate mixed the blood of the people with the sacrifices. He said, "I tell you, . . . unless you repent, you will all likewise perish."

No one in the Bible teaches more about hell than does Jesus. And Jesus taught more about hell than He did about heaven. Yet if there is any teaching of Jesus that the church does not believe, it is His teaching about this dreadful calamity that awaits an impenitent world.

The author of Hebrews, in looking at the vast redemption that has been accomplished for us by Christ, likens us to the people in the Old Testament who for generation after generation ignored God's mercy. They ignored His loving-kindness and grace, to their everlasting peril. The author of Hebrews compares God's mercy in the Old Testament and His mercy in the New Testament. He points out the greater abundance of grace that God pours out upon the world in the gift of Christ in the New Testament and stresses the greatness of the salvation that has been accomplished by Jesus. He then asks a rhetorical question: "How shall we escape if we neglect so great a salvation?" (Hebrews 2:3). Why do I say that question is rhetorical? A rhetorical question is a question for which the answer is obvious. When the author of Hebrews asks, "how shall we escape if we neglect so great a salvation?" the answer is clear. We cannot and we will not escape if we neglect so great a salvation. Escape can result only from repentance and faith. Without these, there is no escape. In logical categories, Jesus said, "Unless you do A, B will inevitably follow. The B is this: You will perish." Repentance is the necessary condition to avoid perishing.

It is dangerous for ministers to tell the public at large that God loves everyone unconditionally. When people hear the term "unconditional love," they think it means, "I can do anything I want, whenever I want, and I never have to worry about God." They assume it means, "I never have to worry about being saved from Him, because His love is unconditional." In one sense, God's love is unconditional, but His salvation is conditional. He requires all people everywhere to repent, to confess their sins, and to despair of any hope of redeeming themselves.

Jesus describes us as debtors. He taught His disciples to pray, "forgive us our debts" (Matthew 6:12). Debtors are people who have an unpaid obligation. You'll remember from chapter 1 that our worldview begins with how we understand the nature of God. At the heart of our understanding of God is the knowledge that God is our Maker and our Ruler. He is sovereign over the human race. God eternally, inherently, and intrinsically has the absolute right to impose obligations upon us. Often we are distressed when someone says we "must" do this or we "ought" to do that. We resist people pointing their fingers at us and telling us what we need to do. They impose a burden of guilt or obligation upon us that we didn't ask for. There are many people who have no authority over me who tell me what I ought to do. But if Almighty God looks at me and says,

"R. C., you ought to do such and such," I cannot argue, because God has the inherent right to impose obligation upon me. The obligation that He has imposed on you and me is the obligation of obedience to His Law. It is that Law that measures the degree of my indebtedness to God.

In our catechism we ask, "What is sin?" The answer is, "Sin is any want of conformity to or transgression of the Law of God." Disobedience to God is an act of lawlessness. Every time we disobey, every time we commit a sin, we incur a debt. The apostle Paul uses a grim image of accrued or amassed guilt:

> And do you think this, O man, you who judge those practicing such things, and doing the same, that you will escape the judgment of God? Or do you despise the riches of His goodness, forbearance, and longsuffering, not knowing that the goodness of God leads you to repentance? But in accordance with your hardness and your impenitent heart you are treasuring up for yourself wrath in the day of wrath and revelation of the righteous judgment of God (Romans 2:3-5).

Echoing the teaching of Jesus that unless we repent we will perish, Paul speaks of our "despising" the riches of God's goodness. That goodness and patience should lead us—indeed it should drive us—to repentance. Instead, His goodness and forbearance become the occasion for the hardening of our hearts. The more people "get away with" sin, the less they tend to worry about its consequences. If we escape the judgment of God for a season, we soon expect to escape it forever.

As we grow more hardened, we become more bold in defying God's law. All the while we do this, the meter is running. Each sin we commit is added to the last one. As we accumulate sin in impenitence, we are creating a storehouse, a treasury of wrath. Paul speaks of "treasuring up" wrath. Usually a treasure is regarded as something desirable. But in this case it is the most dangerous and dreadful surplus anyone can amass.

Paul used this kind of imagery to accentuate our indebtedness to God. Every time I violate the Law of God, I incur a moral debt. Each time I sin, the debt gets larger. Those debts mount up against the day of judgment. The debt becomes so large that I cannot possibly repay it, a situation described in three of Christ's parables (Matthew 18:21-35; Luke 7:40-42; 16:1-13).

The pagan worldview of our culture may grant that nobody is perfect—although perfection itself must be deemed an archaic concept for our culture, since there can be no "perfect" with moral relativism. Still, most people will admit they have done wrong things in their lives. But they judge themselves "on balance." They believe, like Muslims, that if their good deeds outnumber or outweigh their failures, they will enter paradise. They fail to see that God requires perfection. If we sin once, there is no possible way that we can do enough to make up for that one transgression. In our humanness, we hold to a moral "entitlement" program by which it is assumed that everyone is entitled to one mistake. I don't know where this axiom came from. God certainly never entitled us to one sin. Yet even if He did entitle us to a single sin, how long ago did we use up that entitlement?

JESUS HAS PAID OUR DEBT

Seventy percent of people in the United States have credit card debt. They are in over their heads. A friend of mine owes more on her credit card than she makes in a year. She has no hope of ever being able to pay off that debt. Likewise, the sinner who has sinned against God has absolutely no hope of paying off his debt. That is what the gospel is about. It is about God in His mercy. It is about a God who is a God of justice but also a God of grace. He is a God of wrath and also of mercy. We read in the New Testament that God has revealed His grace to us in the gospel—in the doctrine of justification by faith alone. God sent into the world One who incurred no debt, One who lived His entire life in perfect obedience. That's why it is so important for us to understand that Christ is sinless. He came to the end of His life with no debt, and He came to a people who were drowning in debt, who were absolutely impotent to pay the debt, and said, "Give me your debt." He took that debt and He put it on Himself. Paul describes it this way in his letter to the Colossians:

> And you, being dead in your trespasses and the uncircumcision of your flesh, He has made alive together with Him, having forgiven you all trespasses, having wiped out the handwriting of requirements that was against us, which was contrary to us. And He has taken it out of the way, having nailed it to the cross (Colossians 2:13-14).

What a magnificent metaphor to describe the atonement. Paul speaks about letters of indebtedness, certificates of debt. Under Old Testament law, when a person violated the law, it was written down. It was a moral IOU. It produced debtors who could not pay their debts. That's what we are by nature. Paul says that, on the cross, the first thing Christ did in our behalf was to erase the debt. He blotted it out.

Remember David? After his sin with Bathsheba, he was confronted by the prophet Nathan. When he came to a time of real confession, he cried out to God, "blot out all my iniquities" (Psalm 51:9). He was asking God to erase his sins from his record, to expunge them from his history. This is exactly what Christ does for those who put their trust in Him. He blots out the debt.

Then, Paul says, He nails that certificate of debt to the cross. In the ancient world, when a debt was canceled, instead of writing "Paid in full," a Greek figure of a cross was placed on the document. God literally puts a cross over our debt when we repent and embrace Christ.

Who can possibly measure the graciousness of that grace? The mercy of that mercy? This is salvation in the ultimate way—to imagine that Christ has canceled our debt forever and has won for us the forgiveness of every one of our sins. Not only that, He has transferred to our account the perfection of His righteousness for all who believe. When God does that, He does not stop being holy or righteous. Paul says the gospel shows us that God is both "just and the justifier" of those who believe in Christ (Romans 3:26). He never negotiates His righteousness. He makes sure that guilt is punished and that sin is paid for. He doesn't just forgive the debt, He marks it "paid," so that He is still just. He allows it to be paid by Jesus Christ His Son rather than by us, showing forth the glory of His justice and the unspeakable treasure of His grace.

In the final analysis, that which defines the Christian

worldview is the glory of the cross. The cross remains the symbol for all that is loved and embraced in the Christian worldview. It is also the symbol for all that the pagan worldview despises. The cross is the symbol that causes worlds to collide. It provokes a war that will not end until the consummation of the Kingdom of God.

Epilogue:
Resolve in Warfare

On December 7, 1941, American military leaders were shocked, embarrassed, and crushed in spirit by the devastation of our naval fleet at Pearl Harbor. Japanese military leaders were intoxicated with elation at their overwhelming triumph in the sneak attack. It was reported, however, that Admiral Isoroku Yamamoto was less optimistic with the results. He is said to have warned his comrades, "I fear we have awakened a sleeping giant and filled him with a terrible resolve."[5]

"A terrible resolve." It is one thing to pass a resolution

by which certain action is to be taken, or to make a New Year's resolution by which we promise to do a particular thing. Such resolutions are mere statements of intent. We know which road is paved with good intentions, and that the life expectancy of a New Year's resolution is not long.

Making resolutions is quite different from being resolute. To be resolute is to go beyond mere intent. It is to be filled with determination. A "terrible resolve" is one that does not easily fade away, that doesn't cease until the determined end is met. The terrible resolution that Yamamoto feared, ended on the deck of the battleship *Missouri* with the unconditional surrender of the Japanese—a surrender rendered certain by the grim experience of two gigantic mushroom clouds at Hiroshima and Nagasaki.

The United States was involved in World War II for almost four years. It was a time of sacrifice, of rationing, and of heroism at home and abroad. It was the time of Audie Murphy and Rosie the Riveter. We saved grease, tin cans, tin foil, and a host of other things to support the war effort. We grew our own vegetables in the ubiquitous "Victory Gardens." In a word, we were a nation gripped by resolve.

When President Bush called upon the nation to maintain its resolve in the war against terrorism, he knew that when people lose their resolve, they lose their wars. Terrorists count on the civilian population that suffers under their attacks to be unable to maintain a resolute warfare against them. They understand the difference between a war of conquest and a war of attrition.

What is the difference between these types of war? Perhaps the easiest way to explain the difference is to take a brief look at the American Civil War. When hostilities broke out in 1861, it was widely assumed in the North that the war would be over in weeks if not in days. No one expected that 700,000 American lives would be lost in the conflict. It is recorded that, at the Battle of Bull Run, fashionably dressed women rode in carriages near the battle site to watch what they erroneously assumed would be the certain swift victory of the Northern troops. The South was agrarian; the North was industrialized. The money, the armaments, the railroads (until Stonewall Jackson stole Northern locomotives in a daring raid on Harpers Ferry), all heavily favored the North.

What was overlooked was that, while the North was involved in a war of conquest, the South was involved in a war of attrition. For the North to win, they had to conquer and occupy the South, to keep the Southern states from successfully seceding from the Union. For the South to win, they did not have to conquer or occupy a single square foot of Northern real estate. Their goal was simply to hold out until the North lost their resolve to continue waging war.

The South came within a whisker of winning the war of attrition. By the spring of 1863, the civilian population of the North was totally exhausted and disgusted by the war. They were devastated by the loss of hundreds of thousands of their young men. The political pundits gave Abraham Lincoln little chance of being reelected. Resolve to continue fighting was rapidly waning. The South, meanwhile, maintained their resolve, for they were fighting for their homes, their fields, and their way of life.

Fortunately for the North, the tide turned within a super-critical twenty-four-hour period between the Union victory at Gettysburg and the fall of Vicksburg. Perhaps, if not probably, had the South won Gettysburg, they would have won their battle of attrition.

In more recent times we saw a similar case in the warfare between the prodigious power of the United States military and the tiny half-of-a-country, North Vietnam. The North Vietnamese won their war of attrition. They outlasted the resolve of the American government and American people.

To maintain resolve in a civil war or in a world war is a different matter from maintaining resolve in a war against terrorism. In the first six months following 9/11, the nation went through the throes of pain and anger, and there was a surge of patriotism. Stores quickly sold out of American flags. Indeed, citizens displayed more flags in their yards, on their cars, even in lapel buttons, than we have seen since World War II. However, in recent months the number of flags being displayed has been dramatically reduced. The surge of resolve has passed, perhaps waning until another attack against us.

As this resolve dissipates, one wonders if a return to normalcy will signal a return to moral relativism. Will we, as dogs who return to their vomit (Proverbs 26:11; 2 Peter 2:22), reinstate macroevolution as our national anthropology? I hope not. But as long as the Christian worldview is surrounded by pagan and barbarian worldviews, the war of ideas will continue and worlds will continue to collide.

We rejoice that no mortal has the resolve that God Himself has. He is supremely resolute in His determinate counsel to ensure the final triumph of the truth of Christ.

NOTES

1. Jean-Paul Sartre, *Being and Nothingness* (New York: Philosophical Library, 1956), part 4, chapter 2.
2. Will Durant, *The Story of Philosophy* (New York: Simon and Schuster, 1953), 58.
3. Albert Einstein, in a letter to Max Born, December 4, 1926, quoted in Elizabeth Knowles, ed., *The Oxford Dictionary of Quotations* (Oxford: Oxford University Press, 1999), 290.
4. Widely attributed; source unknown.
5. Widely attributed; source unknown.

General Index

abortion, 59

Ahab, 13

American Civil Liberties Union, 28

American civil religion: central axiom of, 17; and culture, 57-63; and God's wrath, 63-67

Amtrak accident (1993), 73

Aristotle, 26, 27

atonement, 80-83

"Battle Hymn of the Republic," 65, 67-68

Bush, George W., 9-10, 86

Caiaphas, 43

Calvinism, 31

capitalism, 11

Catholicism, 14

Christianity, 31; distinction from Judaism, 15-17

Churchill, Winston, 11

Civil War, 10, 87-88

Clinton, Bill, 62

communism, 11

conflict of ideas, 10-12

cross, the, 42, 83. *See also* atonement

David, 53, 81-82

deism, 26-28, 29, 31

"Do your own thing" slogan, 58-59, 62

Durant, Will, 27

ecumenism, 12-13, 14-15

education, "neutral," 27

Einstein, Albert, 46

either/or fallacy, 49

Elijah, 18

finitum non capax infiniti, 39

Galileans slaughtered by Pilate, 72-74, 75

God, 32-33, 38; blessings of, 29-31; as "clock maker," 26; exclusive worship of, 14; and human agency, 32-36; human indebtedness to, 75-80; sovereignty of, 31-32; as

Scripture Index